TRIUMPH HOUSE
Poetry with a Purpose

INSPIRED VOICES

Edited by

CHRIS WALTON

First published in Great Britain in 1998 by
TRIUMPH HOUSE
1-2 Wainman Road, Woodston,
Peterborough, PE2 7BU
Telephone (01733) 230749

All Rights Reserved

Copyright Contributors 1998

HB ISBN 1 86161 399 7
SB ISBN 1 86161 394 6

FOREWORD

Inspired Voices is a carefully crafted anthology of the thoughts, feelings and emotions of over 130 new and established poets of today. Each author holds the special gift of being able to share their own views on life and the world around them in a way that conveys their message to others.

The poems inside vary in style, form and content but all communicate directly with the reader. With a wide variety of views and opinions this is a special collection of poetry that you'll return to time after time.

Chris Walton
Editor

CONTENTS

Joyriders	Rebecca Radley	1
Remember Animals Are Little People In Fur Coats	Jennifer Polledri	2
Untitled	Stephen Baird	4
Tiger	Sandra Houghton	5
Unlucky	S J Haggerty	6
The Sixties	Jean Smith	7
Your Driving Test	Maria Anne Buswell-Davies	8
Bridlington Beach	Margaret Terry	9
Cats	Jenny Anderson	10
The Lure Of The North	Elizabeth Harris	11
The Careful Woman	Margaret Budgen	12
A Cry For Help	Leanne Davidson	13
Seascape	John Alexander	14
The Grieving Widow	J Higginbottom	15
Ireland	Kathleen Johnson	16
The Search For Peace	N H Greenslade	18
Homesickness	Maggie Purr	19
Your Dad	Sarah Kaye Martin	20
Empire	Pippa Lovell	21
Portrait Of The Heart	Jean Carter	22
Ode To A Princess	Jennifer Vrahimis	23
Untitled	Andrew Spencer	24
Alex	Pamela Considine	25
Everyone's Life	Andrew Roy	26
Autumn	Ruth Harman	27
Tranquillity	Margaret Paterson	28
Remember Me	A Benzie	29
A Happier New Year	J A Phillips	30
Childhood Joys	Jonathan Russell	31
Pathways Of Life	T Duggan	32
For Once	Joy Walker	33
My Little Friend, Patch	Elizabeth Collins	34
A Little Bit Of Heaven	Mary-Ann Adams	35
Dinosaurs	Jamie Kirk	36
Picturesque - Historical London	Pam D Jewell	37

Decisions	Steve Lewis	38
Sweet Childhood	Penni Nicolson	40
How	Malcolm T Gould	41
The Shrinking Girl	Stuart Le Grice	42
Untitled	Iris Carey	43
What Is Life	M E Preston	44
Wasted Time	Kim Kilpatrick	45
Fulfilled	P A Ebbage	46
You To I	Lorraine Appleyard	47
Away From The City	Albert Crossley Knight	48
Arm In Arm	Janet Scott	49
Clothes For A Disco	Jennifer Brooks	50
Ode To Seriously Cheesed Off Commuters	Nigel Le Gresley	51
Behind The Stone Wall	Jeff Chick	52
My Only One	Cynthia Dale	54
Homeless	S A Johnstone	55
Christmas	C Butler	56
Untitled	Phil Robinson	57
Diana	Jackie Faunch	58
Untitled	P J Whitaker	59
Ryan Daniel Humphreys	S Walker	60
My Neighbour	Carol Harrington-Brice	61
Give Love Today	M Ross	62
Sundown	Monica Gibson	63
All Hallows' Eve	S Beach	64
The Blackbird's Song	Nick Fawcett	65
The Programmer's Life	Peter J McCafferty	66
Time	K Taylor	67
Prison	Stella R Corbett	68
Save Our Planet	Denise Chappell	69
Progress	Christopher Brown	70
Alice	Trudi-Ann Handley	72
Death In The Past	T C Mountney	73
Unfinished	Julie Sanderson	74
Peace . . . N Ireland, Bosnia, Africa, Iraq . . .	John Horley	75
Mount Of Venus	Vivien Thomas	76

The Lonely Old Man	Irma Chester	77
Tomorrow	I Cone	78
Oh Father	Malcolm Mayo	79
Where Empty Means Full	Nick Williams	80
I'm A Big Girl Now	Jean Lloyd Williams	81
Cooking Up Trouble	Carol Smith	82
Red	M J Hughes	83
My Mum	A Brenda Original	84
The Warning	J Sharp	85
Moving	Amy Bennett	86
A Rose	Margaret Appleyard	87
The Children Of Dunblane	D Hester	88
Pollution	James Brockbank	89
Dearest Niece	David Carress	90
An Obsession	Jayne Wherritt	91
Time	John Winston-Smith	92
The Birthday Hour	Gary Walmsley	93
Christmas	Beth Roberts	94
A Child's Bedtime Prayer	Win Slater	95
Posties	Delma Bruce	96
A Mother In Mind	Edna Ball	97
Autumn And Winter Winds	Nora Billington	98
Poor Daddy Long Legs	Kay Clements	99
The Streets Of London	Margaret Hughes	100
Big Ted	J E Goulding	101
The Waiting Game	Kathleen Johnson	102
Platonic Friendship	Mary Elizabeth Bridges	103
I Just Wanted To	Jenny Betchley	104
I Love You Still	Ralph McMurray	105
Heaven's Very Special Child	G L Crowe	106
Psalm Of Hope	Brenda Finegan	107
When	Thomas Victor Healey	108
Golden Heart Entwine	Rhonda Russell	109
Ghost Ships	Scott Turner	110
Untitled	Kathleen Jarvis	111
A Place	Jessica Wright	112
Burden Of Proof	Timm Dorsett	113
Someone Does Care	Ellen Hall	114

The Cycle Of Time	Heather Brown	115
Forever	Jessica Jordan	116
For What We Are About To Receive	Mary Ryab	117
I Didn't Know You Jesus	John Christopher	118
Pipe Of Peace	Dinah Matthew	119
Suck A Lemon!	Kim Montia	120
Feathers	Zoë Ford	121
What Is It?	GIG	122
The Male Perspective	Christine George	123
Each Day As Our Last	Danny Kember	124
Excuses	Don Goodwin	125
Tonight My Words Fall Like Rain	John Dewar	126
When Someone Dies	Hajar Javaheri	128
Remember . . .	Matthew Allen	129
Firestorm	Paul Willis	130
The Best Things In Life	Catherine Wigglesworth	131
Questions, And The Reasons Why	Simon Green	132
British Disease	Edward Graham Macfarlane	133
Robin	Mary Tickle	134
The Dark Horse	L Heatley	135
The Green Lady	Gordon B Bannister	136

JOYRIDERS

Joyriders
Fool-riders
Think they're cool drivers
Spinning
Whizzing
Not really thinking
Laughing
Singing
Not really caring
Speeding
Free-wheeling
Not really looking
Crashing
Smashing
Weren't at all watching
Dying
Killing
Not really feeling?

Rebecca Radley

REMEMBER ANIMALS ARE LITTLE PEOPLE IN FUR COATS

The child tugged at his mother's arm,
His haste was clear to see.
For months he had yearned for this special day
Then, at last, she had answered his plea.

The two of them walked the winding path.
Through puddles cloudy, obscure.
Till they reached a gate, decrepit with age,
then panic - the boy was unsure.

His life was lonely, friends he had none.
His manner, restrained and reserved.
For he was alone in his silent world,
No voices or sounds could be heard.

They laughed at him, taunted and mocked
At this figure so simple and weak.
Though his intelligence ranked above others,
Some thought him submissive and meek.

He had come to find a friend in need.
Someone who understood.
A being, perhaps who has suffered as he.
To find him - if only he could.

The mother and son walked tirelessly past
rows of animals sadly neglected.
Those creatures' eyes lacked brightness and hope,
for they knew they had all been rejected.

Then swiftly he saw her, curled in a ball,
trying to comfort her puppies.
A desperate young dog, scruffy and wide-eyed.
Defiant, her back to the wall.

She blinked at him in the winter sunlight,
and saw he was friend, not foe.
Then came to the bars and licked his hand.
Soon their friendship began to grow.

The boy glanced up at his mother's face
as a smile softened her features.
He loved her more than ever before
for home he was taking these creatures.

Now his day's filled with happiness,
joy and gladness.
His future was empty no more
These wonderful beings no longer neglected
for them, he had opened a door.

A door to a world filled with warmth and love.
Comfort, well-being and ease.
And to him they gave relief from affliction
Now replaced with contentment and peace.

Jennifer Polledri

UNTITLED

The words on this page fall flatly,
Without texture or feeling,
And being words,
They do not truly express
The realm of the heart,
Which, in oft' essential moments,
Will intermingle
With a sprinkling of reason
To create,
Confusion.

Stephen Baird

TIGER

Sleek stripes slinking through the night,
Ears alert, eyes bright
Pierce through the gloaming, glistening.
Moving silently on measured tread
Pausing, sniffing, ever listening
The tiger seeks, relentlessly on the prowl.
No prior warning to his prey
until a throaty growl, pierces the darkest
nightly sounds of his domain.
Too late! His hunter's instinct rarely fails,
Tonight a jungle lord will eat.
When fully feasted, without a care,
will sleep away the daylight hours.
Awaken, if you dare!

Sandra Houghton

UNLUCKY

Two little ducks, twenty two; that's what they used to say.
Now it's 'All the twos - twenty two,' very upmarket today!
Modern seating, uniformed staff asking 'Would you like some
                                              change, Miss?'
'No I'd like to win,' I murmur with a hiss.
Plum ladies with armless shirts, shoving coins into a slot,
Prize bingo, so much fun, but costs a flamin' lot.
''Ere you are,' shouts one old dear, on her face a pleasant smile,
By this time I'm in a rage, my stomach full of bile.
My 'lucky' pen has let me down, as I wait for number one -
Yes, Kelly's eye is all I need - oh, what jolly fun.
I wait with baited breath as the caller says with glee,
The lucky number for today is number thirty three!

S J Haggerty

THE SIXTIES

Thick platform shoes - we couldn't walk
Our skirts frilled out a mile
And even men wore beads galore
On every face a smile
'I love you' we all called out
The hippies called back loud
'And we love you.' Look at the sky
It's blue. Ignore that cloud
It was an airy fairy world
No drugs or fights or crime
We really let the world sail by
We really had a time
We all sang love songs by the score
Love, peace, were our main goals
We hadn't time to worry
Three cheers for rock an' roll
The sun shone out - we laughed at rain
No face was worried, dour
'Twas all the time 'Be happy folks
Life's full of flower power'

Jean Smith

YOUR DRIVING TEST

Get in that car and think you're a cert,
From the very word go, be completely alert,
Remember your mirror, your gears, your ignition
Get yourself into a most comfortable position.
Your highway code is all a jumble in your head!
It was all straight in your mind when you went to bed.
Now you are on the road, don't forget to stop on red
Just take things easy and keep your confidence flowing
And you will soon find that those nerves are all going.
Do not overtake on a blind bend,
Drive to your utmost and set a good trend!
We know you will sail through it, because you have what it takes.
But don't be too hasty when using those brakes!
Those lessons have paid off now for you have passed your test.
The instructor beside you has made his decision
And gives you a golden hand-shake for driving
with such accuracy and precision.
Your nerves have all gone now, and you feel so swell
You have got your certificate, so tear up those L's.

Maria Anne Buswell-Davies

BRIDLINGTON BEACH

Chameleon shore remoulded constantly
By wind and tide, relentless giants,
Of ever-changing moods.
I tread the variable tide-line day by day,
Cloudless blue calm laps glistening sand;
White stones piled high by elemental force;
Shells for the picking; seaweed in great swathes -
Plastic waste bottles and corroding cans
Tangled line and broke lobster pots . . .
. . . Grey mist, rain-bearing clouds and angry waves,
White-crested gnawing at the beach -
Threatening gradually collapsing cliffs
Where mini landslides mingle mud with sand . . .
. . . Or winter evenings when the sky turns pink and gold,
And black gulls circle over silver sea,
And solid stubborn mass of cliff grows dark . . .
Then lure of tea and sheltered warmth of fire
Draws me and guesting dogs plodding up slope
Towards home.

Margaret Terry

CATS

Tabitha the tabby cat lived inside the barn
Manx the puss without a tail came out from the farm
Abigail the tortoiseshell was a proud new mum
Kittens tumbled everywhere playing in the sun
for a while Henry hound sat and watched them there
Soon he got up hot and tired
Slumped beneath a chair
By eve the cats went inside
Supper saucers were all laid
Filled with fish and milk that
Tom the farmer saved
At night the owl came out
To watch beneath the hunter's moon
Till dawn came with the blackbirds
And their cheery tune.

Jenny Anderson

THE LURE OF THE NORTH

There's magic on a highland shore,
Stretching as far as the eye can see.
Endless golden sand, who'd ask for more?
Here is solitude for you and me!

Unfrequented beaches, round our coast,
Where we can wander, from end to end,
For perfect peace, this is the utmost -
Untroubled, tranquil days to spend.

On the near islands, sheep are grazing,
A homing fishing boat comes into sight -
On a rocky bay, seals are basking,
Noiseless are the seagulls in their flight.

We feel old troubles have never been,
Imagined worries just drift away,
And marvel at the sights we have seen,
Look forward, with joy, to each new day!

Roaming on these shores, we've often been,
Our love for our country will never wane.
Once home, will recall each precious scene,
Know that, someday we'll be there again!

Elizabeth Harris

THE CAREFUL WOMAN

She refused tobacco and cholesterol;
She exercised, paid gym club fees;
Careful, she practised weight control
According to medical expertise,
She didn't die of heart disease.

Stress was out; she didn't consume
Salt and caffeine, not even Coke.
She regularly danced and walked
And avoided other people's smoke.
She didn't die of a stroke.

She didn't lie out in the sun;
She used a sun block - took no chances;
She had X-rays and smears and scans,
Always receiving the right answer.
No, she didn't die of cancer.

She took such care behind the wheel
Of her checked and serviced English Ford.
She didn't speed or drink and drive;
She studied well the highway code.
She didn't die upon the road.

Additives, chemicals, none were allowed;
She only ate organic produce;
She always said 'No' to addictive drugs
And exercised her right to refuse.
She didn't die of drug abuse.

Today she's deaf and nearly blind.
Her mind's confused; she's filled with rage.
Legs are painful, hands are weak.
Her body has become a cage.
Now she's dying of old age.

Margaret Budgen

A Cry For Help

Life is not all that it seems,
I think, stare and dream so many dreams.
Thinking I don't have feelings like all of you,
The restrictions, the madness, that's why I'm so blue.
So the let downs and surprises just fall into place,
Look at me, the love, the hatred, you can see it in my face.
Friendships, caring, a bit of love here and there,
That's all I need from someone somewhere.
Maybe an angel will come soon, one day,
To rescue me, and take me far, far away.

Leanne Davidson

SEASCAPE

Walls of water, houses high,
Reaching for a troubled sky,
Pause, then lean and fall.

Winds that tear and chew and bite
All day long and through the night,
As gale and storm and squall.

Rain and mist and brief sunlight
Before the curtain of the night
Begins its seaward fall.

A faint horizon, dull and grey,
Beckoning lights from in a bay,
For trawler, ship and yawl.

Calm water and a wind that's light,
Tucked up for a stormy night
Behind the harbour wall.

John Alexander

THE GRIEVING WIDOW

She sits all alone
With unseeing eyes
You'd think she were dead
If it weren't for her sighs
Tears falling softly
Slowly at first
The start of relief
For a heart fit to burst
Her words are so bitter
She speaks to the night
'Why did you leave me?
Who gave you the right?
You left me so quickly
No kiss, no goodbyes.
Surely you knew
I would never survive
And now will I live
Friendless years ahead
And long loveless night
Alone in my bed.'
But in her despair
She remembers his pain
She'd loved him too well
To want that again.
Now there's calm in her eyes
With hope her heart fills
Soon she'll be with him
For loneliness kills.

J Higginbottom

IRELAND

Who will man the barricade of peace?
Who will carry the flag of peace?
For the cause of liberty so that
Ireland might be free.
Will that be you? You and me.

Who will man the barricade of peace?
Who will carry the flag of peace?
With the children of the brave. Who
Have died for liberty, so that
Ireland might be free.
Will that be you? You and me.

Or will you turn your face away,
When you hear their children cry,
As they watch their fathers die
For the cause of liberty so that
Ireland might be free?
Will that be you? You and me.

While the world looks on in vain
And say England is to blame and
We hang or heads in shame.
Will that be you? You and me.

Or will we man the barricade of peace?
Will we carry the flag of peace
With the children of the brave
Who have died for liberty so that
Ireland might be free?

Will we see them live and grow?
Will we see them laugh and play?
Will we dry their children's tears?
Will we take them by the hand?
Will we see their children smile
as they build a better land
For the children of the brave
who have died for liberty so that
Ireland might be free?
Will that be you? You and me.

Kathleen Johnson

THE SEARCH FOR PEACE

A vandalised park bench;
Smiles from a toothless alcoholic,
A stray collie runs;
An ice-cream dropped,
A child's tears shine;
A hurried word is lost.
Be decided, push at the heavy door.
The hallway is dark
The benches empty,
Footsteps echo on stone.
Jesus was here
A long time ago.
I sit before a huge crucifix;
I have found peace.

I stand before the door
What is it you want?
I search for peace
Come in, my son, come in.

N H Greenslade

HOMESICKNESS

Other world,
Tears are soaking me through,
Endless crying for the fear of all things new,
Wet tissue -
Crumpled in my lonely hand.
Shaken.

Mascara blots and rash-raw clots,
Wishing wells and forget-me-nots,
Tidal tears come in waves at every
surge of morbid thought.
Shaking.

Memories,
I understand my sacrifice now,
But it's too late for asking how?
I must kiss my photos, my pictures
my letters, my little toys - that they bought
      with a good luck thought - Goodbye.
Thinking.

Am I sinking?
Write down all I have,
All I have now is this,
And a faintly fading kiss,
I can talk to many faces but still sense
silence in my heart,
Loneliness on my part.

Sighing.
Perhaps torment subsides with time,
Then the sun will shine.

Maggie Purr

YOUR DAD

Scourge of weeds
Planter of seeds
Mower of lawn
Saw you born
Tier of laces
Pulls funny faces
Singer of songs
Righter of wrongs
Repairer of tyres
Builder of bonfires
Sticker of plasters
Sorts out disasters
Teller of tales
Calmer of wails
Have no doubt
The loudest shout
Cuddles up tight
Kisses night-night
Carries you to bed
Strokes sleepy head
He's woodland guide
Shoulder ride
Barbecue chef
Argument ref
Chaser of ghosts
Who beams and boasts
That's my girl over there
Green eyes and golden brown hair
Your dad's face lights up as he watches you play
He loves us and we love Dad, no more to say.

Sarah Kaye Martin

EMPIRE

Sacred knowledge of a forgotten tribe,
Secrets and mysteries they hide.
Hidden truths lie undiscovered,
Inscriptions and scrolls slowly being uncovered.

Mexico is their homeland,
Where temples and pyramids stand
Guarding what is rightfully theirs,
Worshipping the gods who cared.

A completely different culture.
Palenque is what I see.
Finding out about their residence,
Knowing there's more evidence.

Archaeologists trying to find vital clues,
Uncovering ancient tombs.
Pyramids stand so tall,
The chambers like rooms.

The Mayan's knowledge so advanced
To understand fully, there's not much chance.
What a life they must lead,
To know the secrets and mysteries.

One thing that angers me,
Disturbing the tombs of buried people and jewels,
Will bring unhappiness and anger to the gods,
Have they no respect at all?

Pippa Lovell

PORTRAIT OF THE HEART

To write a poem, to bare your soul
And empty it of all it holds
Passion, love, hate or fear
To write sweet words of someone dear.
Or rid your hurting, bitter heart
The hatred of someone
Or try to find compassion
For each and everyone.
If that it should rhyme or not
And words make little sense
Does it matter - Not a jot!
- Of no consequence.
Troubled mind can cloud the score -
Think again and think still more.
Search each corner of your mind
Untold treasures you may find.
Let your thoughts flow as they will
From the very start
Emotions deep will really show
The portrait of your heart.

Jean Carter

ODE TO A PRINCESS

The world could not be more aggrieved
By the senseless death causing many bereaved;
But God has his plan for our Princess dear
For her with God's children to be near.

In Heaven and on Earth, our brightest star
Shines so brightly, nothing can mar
The seeds of goodness Diana did sow;
They'll blossom and flourish and around the world flow.

Those acts of kindness, humility and love
Were for Diana like a hand to a glove;
The world's tribute, I'm sure all will say
Is to carry on her good deeds - day by day.

Jennifer Vrahimis

UNTITLED

Hush now, hey now.
I put a curse on you.
From now until the end of time
All for the things you do.

I curse you by the stream and brook,
I curse you for the love you took.
I curse you as the wild dogs bark.
Open your eyes - don't see in the dark.

You built me up, you knocked me down.
You made me feel a clown.
The pleasure you had in leaving me!
My tear-stained eyes just drown.

How do you think I will survive
Now that I have no mate?
I'll tell you what I'll feast upon,
A diet of pure hate!

In the beginning we laughed so much
And the flame of joy danced free.
But I wasn't given to knowing
That one day you'd laugh at me.

Shall I be so bitter all my life?
My rainy days are wet.
You may have forgotten me,
But I may forget you yet.

Andrew Spencer

ALEX

I haven't known you very long
You are really very new
But from the moment you came along
My love just grew and grew
Your little face so cute
Your mouth just like a rose
Two big blue eyes a button for a nose
From the moment that I saw you
I have loved you more and more
Your smiles and gurgles are a joy
As soon as I walk through the door
Each day becomes a pleasure
And I hope for many more
To love and play with my little treasure

Pamela Considine

EVERYONE'S LIFE

Lives flash past
other people, creatures, carrying out
unusual, everyday tasks.

Nothing is familiar as it fits
awkwardly into place.
Nothing and everything makes perfect nonsense.

Strange actions, activities executed as normal
everything is familiarly unusual,
recognisably different, perfectly spoiled.

All actions, motions have meaning,
routinely unpredictable.
Life is strange in its peculiar normality.

Strange as it seems,
life is straightforwardly complicated.

Andrew Roy

AUTUMN

I walked into the dew sprayed field
And was struck by an amazing sight.
For right in the middle of a soft carpet of grass
I caught a glimpse of golden light
And a flash of viridian.
A sweet, sweet smell hit my nose
And fascination forced me to impose
My presence at this beautiful scene.

So I walked up to the golden light
And saw that it was leaves.
The flash of viridian was apples
And I took a chance to seize
A rich, ripe apple from the tall bronze tree
And hold it tight, close to me.

Ruth Harman

TRANQUILLITY

Tranquillity comes, with the early morning walk,
when your spirits soar, like the gliding hawk.
Down a woodland path, 'neath a leafy glade,
you're at peace with the world, and your tensions fade.

The sun streaks through each hanging bough,
where the young buds are bursting to new life now,
and the sweet clear sounds of the birds on high,
fill your heart with delight, as you hear their cry.

And the babbling brook, at the foot of the hill,
makes such lovely music, that you feel the thrill,
of the joy of life, as it flows through your veins,
at the beauty you see, as you walk down the lanes.

Then refreshed, you return, to your task in life,
be you husband, or child, or busy wife,
sure of the fact, that as each day dawns,
the beauty of nature will inspire you on.

Margaret Paterson

REMEMBER ME

Sadness, loneliness, left in your despair
All because those around you haven't a care
What does it matter that you live
In forced isolation by a society who doesn't care
Long outlived your purpose
Long outlived your use

Where now are your children dependent
Long absent, some dead
Your only solace lay in prayer and bed
Winter a hateful reaper
Gas bills and electricity get no cheaper
But who is to be your keeper?

None come forth, they're all too busy
Unable to stop, wrapped up in their own complacent lives
Eyes closed as yours soon will be
And who will remember you?

A Benzie

A HAPPIER NEW YEAR

Away with the old, ring in the new
Resolutions made, time to start anew
Sad moments left behind, courage to begin again
Although cruel doubts remain

No-one knows what the future may bring
Make the most of everything
Don't put off until tomorrow the things to do today
Take opportunity by the hand if it comes your way.

In our busy lives with little time to spare
A few kind words, a smile, just to show you care
Never take for granted all that you hold dear
Pause and think of others for a happier new year.

J A Phillips

CHILDHOOD JOYS

Sticky sweets, sherbert dabs, slab toffee and gob stoppers
These cannot be found by today's modern shoppers,
Broken biscuits in a cone of the *Evening News,*
Little trays of goodies for little boys to choose
Thick rashers of bacon sliced while you wait
And if you are short of cash, there is always the slate.
Schoolboys flicking fag cards, lined against a wall
Shouts of triumph when they made them fall
Whipping tops with string tied to a stick
Playing knock down Ginger was a favourite trick
Bowling iron hoops along were fun times
Especially when they got stuck in those tram lines
Hopscotch kept the girls hopping on one leg
They got down the course quicker than boiling an egg
Happy days filled with pleasures of all kinds
There was no television then to poison our minds.

Jonathan Russell

PATHWAYS OF LIFE

Living life to the limit
Enjoying every day
Taking easy strides
Let nothing in your way
If you find your path is blocked
By something on the ground
There will always be another route
You just have to look around
Another way to be chosen
But only for the strong
Not for those too scared to change
Or too weak to carry on
Those who are too tired
To take the longer road
Will not enjoy the freedom
Of the life that they are owed
They settle for contentment
While others search for fun
Growing old too quickly
While the years are still so young
But those who are still willing
To fight the troubles and strife
Can look forward to the future
Of an eventful happy life.

T Duggan

For Once

Why do I feel so alone,
though surrounded by my family at home.
Talking, laughing all around,
but loneliness can still be found.
I so much want to talk to you,
but you always seem to have things to do.
Is a simple phone call too much to ask,
and talking to me such a task?

But yet when we're alone you still,
treat me as if to you I thrill.
Then you, for days, I never see,
you don't know what this does to me.
The laughter and love that we could share
for once, for me I wish you'd be there.

Joy Walker

My Little Friend, Patch

We stroll each day through the grass and trees
We love the misty rain and gentle breeze
Your black ears pricked up, nose to the ground
You search for new scents, listen for sounds

You stand very still, tail in the air
What's that noise - a bird, cat or hare?
Here comes your friend, a biscuit in his pocket
Forgetting scents and sounds, you run to him like a rocket

We sit and listen to the blackbirds sing
And the laughter of children as they soar on their swings
Dogs pass by and you bark in greeting
Through you, a lot of new friends I'm meeting

You stay close by now, you're not too brave in the dark
It's time once more to leave this lovely park
Tired feet, weary paws, trod home once more
Oh little friend, Patch, it's nice to see our own front door.

Elizabeth Collins

A LITTLE BIT OF HEAVEN

Give me a little bit of heaven.
See that red sky that glows so bright,
Just feel the wind softly blowing,
That very light breeze at night.

Stand on a lake so still,
With those reflections that can be seen
The night is so still,
It feels so serene.

Give me a little bit of heaven,
Being with someone you love,
Sitting in a boat on a lake,
Looking at those stars above.

Give me a little bit of heaven,
Up there looks so grand,
Give me a little bit of heaven,
Come on, take my hand.

Mary-Ann Adams

DINOSAURS

Dinosaurs are creatures which evolved millions of years ago,
I think plesiosaurus is a relative of Nessie, but others just say no.
The triceratops has horns on its forehead and on its nose
The carnivores and vegetarians are really deadly foes.
T-rex is the largest dinosaur of the lot,
And it and the pterandon frequently fought.
They vanished about 65 million years ago
Why they went, nobody really knows.

Jamie Kirk (11)

PICTURESQUE - HISTORICAL LONDON

London is a place of history, of national heritage
It enthrals the young and old alike
The River Thames especially
Gives out a message of its own
You can sense a feeling of peace and calm
It makes you feel tranquil
There are all the river boats
That people go on every day

To see the great Thames barrier
To visit places like Kew Gardens, Hampton Court
Richmond Park, Greenwich and the Cutty Sark
Then there are all the museums to visit
Where knowledge of the past we gain

Both Westminster Abbey and St Paul's Cathedral
Are a wondrous joy to go inside
Praise can be given to the Lord for our very lives
The shops of London, too, are a wondrous sight
Displaying all their wares with great delight

There's London Zoo, of course
Where all the animals can be seen
The parks of London in the summer do invite us
The trees with all their branches, and green, green grass
The flowers in full bloom
Varying colours to be seen
The different kinds of wildlife, like the little squirrel
Look so beautiful to all who pass their way

We must not leave out the restaurants
For without them, where would people be
There is a daily need for food and drink
There's never a dull moment in London
For there's always plenty to do and see.

Pam D Jewell

DECISIONS

Decisions, decisions, decisions you find
Are the things that you make when you make up your mind.

I must get up! We've all said it before,
No, I think I'll just have a few minutes more.

I'm now out of bed and sat on a chair,
Now to decide which clothes I should wear.

Should I go for a run to keep myself thin?
Oh, it's cold and raining, so I think I'll stay in.

I go to the kitchen for something to eat,
Maybe muesli or cornflakes or even puffed wheat?

I travel to work anyway that I like,
I could walk, go by bus or even by bike.

When lunch time comes, I have to decide,
Do I eat at work or go home for the ride?

When work is done and I've got my pay,
Do I go straight home or stop on the way?

On arrival at home it's time for tea,
Do I microwave one minute or make it three?

I sit down to watch the shows on the box,
I think I'd rather be sorting my socks!

It's time for bed! I think with a smile,
Should I go to sleep or read for a while?

So whatever we do, we make up our minds.
Using knowledge and wisdom and thoughts of all kinds.

Yesterday's choices you made so fast,
can change your life in a way that will last.

Sometimes for better and sometimes for worse,
So please be careful as you read this verse.

And take your time to choose what to do,
'Cause the rest of your life is up to you!

Steve Lewis

Sweet Childhood

Ah! sweet childhood when life seemed all aglow,
When there were never in-betweens, only sun or snow,
When fear was only an adult whim, to be sniffed and let go.
Ah! Sweet childhood - I did not know.

Ah! Sweet childhood when life seemed all ablaze,
With dandelions and buttercups, and innocent childish ways,
When bees flew by without a sting, in the glinting sunlight rays,
Ah! Sweet childhood, what tricks you played.

Ah! Sweet childhood, when life seemed brave and bold,
When reality was Santa Claus, and you did not mind the cold,
When in the glow of firelight - the shadows, stories told.
Ah! Sweet childhood, as good as gold.
Ah! Sweet childhood, pity growing old.

Penni Nicolson

How

How peaceful walking on a lonely hill,
On a cold, crisp winter's morning.
Looking down at the countryside so still,
Dawn silently breaks forth, the birds start singing.

False lighting fades, life gathers speed,
While you still can breathe fresh air,
Thoughts of work and family need,
Oh, how much you really care.

You strain your eyes trying to see,
Your home where your family dwell
The place where you used to be,
Praying that your children are well.

Peace and friendship should be our aim,
The fear of violence is always near,
Time to quell the hungry flame.
Then from within, our hearts' love will appear.

Malcolm T Gould

THE SHRINKING GIRL

There was a girl whose name was Jane
One day she got caught in the rain
Her mother said, 'Quick, come inside
Your clothes are damp,' 'They're not,' Jane lied
Jane stayed outside and had some fun
Until the rain gave way to sun
And very soon the puddles dried
Which upset Jane - she nearly cried
She didn't though, she only sighed
And said 'Oh, well, I'll go inside.'
But when she walked up to the door
She was quite shocked by what she saw
The door was huge, doubled in size
Poor Jane could not believe her eyes
She quickly gave her mum a shout
She'd know what this was all about
Mum said, ' I know what's happened here,
The rain has shrunk you, my poor dear,
I've seen it happen to a shirt,
But never a girl. Did it hurt?'
Jane said 'It didn't hurt at all,
But I don't like being this small'
For Jane it was not over yet,
She shrunk each time that she got wet,
And so she could not bathe or wash,
And soon she smelled like eggs gone-off,
So, if you play out in the rain
You should remember poor, small Jane
She stayed out playing in a squall
And now, alas, is far too small.

Stuart Le Grice

UNTITLED

I've seen the darkness float away
To become another day
I've watched the sun from early morn
Like a fireball to be born
To light the darkness
That surrounds the earth
To do goodness of its worth
For sunshine brings eternal glow of light
Till the day turns into night

Iris Carey

WHAT IS LIFE

It's good to help along life's way
Not leave until another day.
Someone may need your help, so stay -
Please listen, do not turn away.

The good Samaritan in you
Could give a lift to one who knew
The depths and degradation too
With a quiet word, just from you.

Perhaps you might need someone's ear
One day along the way, to cheer
You up and listen to you here.
Just a kindness, someone will hear.

You could go along life's way
Ignoring all on every day.
Peace and love in your heart? I say
Compassion must be there to stay.

What is life without a friend?
Nothing!

M E Preston

WASTED TIME

Is she back?
Is the bubble about to burst?
Is the price her happiness?
Or is it us?

Are you really mine?
Or am I just wasting time?
Will you shoot through when she calls,
Pick up the pieces when she falls?

Shall I give in without a fight?
Let you say goodbye while I say goodnight?
Will I sink while you soar,
Taking with you, my heart as you leave by the door?

I'll fight for you tooth and nail
And then my love, if I fail,
My best I'll have given, no need to hide,
Left with a broken heart, but still my pride

But you, my love, will have tossed away
True happiness, a chance to stay
But this choice is yours to make
Take your time, don't tempt fate.

Once again, my mind runs off
Making mountains out of nought
I know your love is like a river
Flowing endlessly, forever.

Kim Kilpatrick

FULFILLED

I wonder if I'll ever know
the miracle of life,
if I will hold my own dear child
when I become a wife,
I can't imagine how it feels
to feed a babe at breast
to cuddle, love and cherish it,
as birds do in the nest -
Well these were thoughts I pondered on
while just a girl at play
I couldn't wait to grow up
and I wished the years away.
Now I have made it, as I played it
Acquired all these joys
I'm married to a lovely man
and have two precious boys.

P A Ebbage

You To I

If I were to you as you to I
My heart would heave a blissful sigh
My eyes would fill with salty tears
And I could ponder on the years
That you and I would share in bliss
In holding hands, in loving kiss
I often dream as time goes by,
If I am to you, as you to I.

Lorraine Appleyard

AWAY FROM THE CITY

He'd never walked on grass so green
Skies so blue, he'd never seen

Of the things he would see, he had been told
Before him it would all unfold

His life was one of high rise flats
Broken lifts and dogs and cats

Cycle frames and burned out cars
Old settees and plastic jars

Today was one he would remember
From January to December

The country called and so he went
The most glorious day he'd ever spent

What he saw, he wanted more
Because he'd never seen before

A host of golden daffodils
Growing wild upon the hills

Was this real or just a dream?
He'd even paddled in a stream

Trees and flowers, views so great
To see it all, he couldn't wait

That in thought he almost wept
As the memories of the day he kept

He had not seen all he went to see
But what he saw, God had given free.

Albert Crossley Knight

ARM IN ARM

I soar above the sky so bright
Out into the moonlit night
See the flowers, see the trees
Down below me in the breeze.
I'm soaring higher now
Above the rivers, above the streams,
High above the mountain tops.
So peaceful, so calm, someone comes to take my arm.
'Come with me, let's see what we can see,
Up in the higher realms of eternity.'
Beautiful colours shining bright,
Vivid blue, purple and white.
With not another soul in sight, we travel round in the night.
I hear the sound of a distant drum
And someone is beckoning me to come
Nearer and nearer I go to the sound
My friend and I, arms locked, and securely bound
We have come together as one, twin souls.
We reach the sound of the drum beat
And an Indian chief stands to his feet.
So peaceful and so calm, we let go of each other's arm.
'Welcome to the promised land
Please take a drink and sit with me.'
We sit upon the ground, as the bowl is passed around.
So peaceful and so calm, we take each other's arm.
We must return as dawn is breaking through,
'It has been a pleasure meeting you.
Farewell.' We promise to return soon
The sun is now rising and gone is the moon.

Janet Scott

CLOTHES FOR A DISCO

I'm going to a disco
What should I wear?
Should I wear my jeans
or should I just go bare?

I have a little belly top
pink with blue spots
I could have worn it with my jeans
but it shows quite a lot
but when I'm partying all day long
I should get rather hot
So I think I'll wear my jeans
and my little belly top

At the disco, I'm number one
everyone else has dresses on
I swing my hips, I show my gear
because I am certainly the best one here.

Jennifer Brooks (12)

ODE TO SERIOUSLY CHEESED OFF COMMUTERS

A typical day on the London express,
that's Great Eastern line's train of vitesse.
We arrive on time as we have to commute,
we don't take our cars as they tend to pollute.
A hard day ahead with much to be done,
but travelling Great Eastern is really no fun.

I suppose, to give credit, it's often not them
who screw up the service creating mayhem.
It's Rail Track, of course, who supply the line plant.
They think that they can - but really they can't.
With failures of power, of signals and switches,
some major in nature, some temporary glitches.

But all add together to give us real pain,
To travel to work, we must take the train.
Just like British Rail, but slightly up beat,
they have no incentive, no need to compete,
and surface improvements have failed to repair
our company's losses, our stressful despair.

Then late in the day when we're now homeward bound;
when we've plans to go out or have friends coming round,
The same awful service we can guarantee -
from a broken down engine or leaves from a tree,
But one thing's for certain, we've had it to here
with useless excuses that bring us no cheer.

Nigel Le Gresley

BEHIND THE STONE WALL

Forty years ago you were brought here at the age of six, do you remember?
A cardboard suitcase neatly packed, no goodbyes, no kisses,
A man in a black suit held your hand and led you through
The large iron gates that closed behind you,
There, for the first time, you saw the stone wall,
This was to be your only world.

There you stayed, a child locked away, year by year you grew up remembering less,
You stopped talking, now most of your day is spent pacing,
Going nowhere, Hands knotted together, feeling anxious,
Bars on the windows, locks on the doors, screams that go on all night,
Afraid and alone, Pull your blanket tightly around you,
Protect yourself, morning is but a short while away.

Behind the stone wall through all seasons and weathers,
There you sit on the wooden bench, mumbling to imaginary friends
Sometimes you smile, you watch and wait, but for whom?
No-one comes to visit, no-one remembers that you're here,
Silent birthdays come and go. Do you remember, do you care?

Your life has been one long endless day, no holidays and no friends
Except those in your head. A voice shouts 'You're all the same here,
I'm watching you, behave yourselves or else.'
Here you stay, life wasting, growing old, solitary,
You have understanding, a heart, a soul, you must feel, we all do,
Yet you stay locked in your own damaged world,
What would you say if you could?

Unshaven, hair a mess, food stains on your shirt,
Trousers too long, scraping the floor, your boots letting in water,
Have you slowly lost the battle to care for yourself?
What made you so different at the age of six? Who decided your miserable fate for you?
what circumstances brought you here?
Look on, no hope, no future, no choice for you
　. . . Behind the stone wall . . .

Jeff Chick

MY ONLY ONE

I watch the river rushing
I hear children chatter
But I'm empty and sad
What does anything matter?
Nothing seems good
Now my love has gone.
How could this happen
To my *only one*.
The only one who made me young
The only one who gave me life,
The only one who I believed
Would always be worth any strife.
To be with him is everything,
To be with him is all I need.
But sadly he does not need me
So I become like the river's reeds,
They sway and tremble in the breeze
Without the sun they just hang on,
And so my life is much the same,
Without my love, I just hang on.

Cynthia Dale

HOMELESS

I wander these lonely streets
Looking for somewhere to rest
My possessions in a carrier bag
Held closely to my chest
I lay down on my usual bench
And try to rest for the night
To sleep away today's events
Under the cold street light
Is this to be my lifestyle
Will it always be like this
Memories flooding through my head
Memories of the home I miss.

S A Johnstone

CHRISTMAS

That night the snow fell, snow on top of snow.
A night of silence yet from below
A magic came from somewhere deep
beyond the still and dreamless sleep.
Past churchyard yew, the darkest tree
no light reveals its mystery.
Down the street another tree - the one we know -
multicoloured lanterns glow.
The pond, now dark and looks unknown;
water frozen like a stone.
A bird takes flight, the moonlit wings
Further back and farther in.

Her call breaks free;
that's where this story did begin
Further back and farther in.

Around the corner she dips then flies
over the fields, the parallel rise
of the moon keeps pace
until all space - is bright,
(although the village light
is left behind.) Across the snow;
deep, crisp and even, though
she tires, her lungs she fills
and flying high, a song she trills.
The song of hope and peace
we all should know.
If only we could just let go
of all our fear and again begin;
Further back and farther in.

C Butler

UNTITLED

The secret sands of yesterday's shores
leave me gasping for breath,
with an open book in my hand . . .
Do you love me for what I am?
Or for what you think I am?
Or for what you think I am not?

Phil Robinson

DIANA

You were one in a million, so compassionate and true,
You gave love to so many people your whole life through.
It was so freely given which gained you respect and adoration,
You won not only the love of England, but also the hearts of the nation.
Your caring and sharing with the sick young the old,
Just proves your were a true royal princess with a heart full of gold.
We are so full of sorrow that you have had to depart,
But you will be remembered as the Queen of Hearts.
So, rest in peace, as you will hold a very special part,
Deep down within all our hearts.

Jackie Faunch

UNTITLED

Those night-time terrors that wake us with a start,
sweaty palms and a fast beating heart,
unknown troubles beset us too,
then the realisation
that I am alone without you.
I awoke from a dream of some previous life
where laughter's the norm, and joy, not strife
then the chasm of realisation's dawning
I'm alone in my bed with my heart breaking.
Till rest itself becomes the terror,
where present and past are both sides of a mirror,
where we can lose our minds
as well as our senses
it's senseless to fear what's beyond the last door.
The only way forward is just as before.
don't be plagued by the mind's ramblings,
it's the subconscious just keeping score!
So step out in tune with our karma,
each successive day just brings it nearer
it's not the ending of life, just the death of an era,
despite my attempts, I can't make it any clearer.

P J Whitaker

RYAN DANIEL HUMPHREYS
(born 19th January 1997 - died 6th February 1997)

Your tiny hand squeezed my finger tight,
As in the incubator you lay, such a beautiful sight,
A darling baby, so small yet so sweet,
Just ten inches from head to feet.

You brought us joy beyond compare
It's so hard to believe you're no longer here,
But to us you were only to be lent,
So the angels to get you, God soon sent.

Eighteen days and six hours too,
Was all we had to share with you,
Yet we loved you with all our hearts,
And with your memory we will never part.

You're in our thoughts every single day,
Our love for you will never go away,
Every little flower, every drop of rain,
Will have us thinking of you again.

So Ryan, when all tears are shed,
There are no words that can be said,
To ease the pain we both now feel,
By losing our grandson who was so real.

From Nanny & Grandad Walker
with all our love and kisses

S Walker

My Neighbour
(To my neighbour, Gordon)

It's a five minute job, would you like to help,
That's what neighbours are for,
There's the window, the gate, the patio slabs
A wobbly hinge on the door.

Thanks for building the outhouse,
A wonderful job it was too,
There're trees to be cut, a lawn to be mown,
The flush won't work on the loo.

A supporter of Leeds doesn't matter
When there is work to be done,
Remember the tap, a five minute job,
Wasn't that good, healthy fun.

If I win the lottery, you're first in mind,
No money would ever change hands,
A screwdriver set, a bag of cement,
And three bags of builders' sand.

Carol Harrington-Brice

GIVE LOVE TODAY

Everyone needs some kind of loving, with God's special gift,
Offering heartfelt emotion, to give them that extra lift!
Don't put off 'til tomorrow, to tell someone how much you care -
Or it's possible, the chance is, they'll no longer be there!
So the message to us all comes loud and plain,
Give them love today, for yesterday won't come back again!

M Ross

SUNDOWN

As the golden sun sinks slowly,
And you stand in raptured bliss
Seeing it in all its beauty,
feel it give a sunlit kiss.

When the sun sinks like a fire,
All the sky is red and gold.
So its beauty holds you spellbound
Holds you as the night grows cold.

Very soon beyond the sky line,
Will the golden ball sink down.
and 'twill seem Earth's light has vanished,
Like a curtain closing round.

We must wait until tomorrow,
When the sun once more appears,
Count your blessings while you have them
As you journey through your years.

Monica Gibson

ALL HALLOWS' EVE

A normal day, until twilight sets in,
The night of the spirits is about to begin.
It's the night when, in ghosts, people believe,
It's the night of the witches, All Hallows' Eve.

Children parade in their costumes so grand,
Knocking on doors with an expectant hand.
Some dressed in black, like vampire bats,
Some dressed like witches with pointed hats.

Skeletons, ghosts and all kinds of ghouls;
With tridents and masks as their fear striking tools.
Slowly they disappear, one by one,
Pleased with their evening of eerie fun.

I can still hear the echoes of 'Trick or treat'
Up and down our now empty street.
All is quiet, all is still,
Now it's all over, the Hallowe'en thrill.

But deep in the night, what ghouls may stir?
As the storm clouds gather, the stars they blur.
The creatures of the night silently roam;
As the children are safely tucked up at home.

S Beach

THE BLACKBIRD'S SONG

A vibrant sound it was -
Not sickly sweet, nor harsh or shrill,
Yet with an awesome power to thrill;
To stir the heart and touch the soul
And make the wounded spirit whole.
You ask me why? Because
It spoke of priceless gifts -
Of lasting peace and inner joy;
Contentment nothing can destroy;
Of loving life and being free;
Becoming all we're meant to be -
Such thoughts my soul uplifts!
What other moment brings
This calm to soothe the fevered mind,
Dispelling cares of every kind?
Or what so moves our deepest self
Bestowing such amazing wealth,
As when the blackbird sings?

Nick Fawcett

THE PROGRAMMER'S LIFE

For hours he sits studying, thin lines moving fast
his eyes straining to capture the data flowing past
Making sense of all the details other programmers have included
Identifying where the system fails, his experience exuded

Watch closely for it may seem that he appears frozen
in a picture of the scene,
Don't make the mistake of thinking
Nothing's doing anything,
He's busy planning, turning out ideas by the ream,
Transformed into ink-shapes,
On his paper print machine.

Steering a course in trial and error
The task becomes clearer, the coding barer
Deserted data lies redundant,
Growing in piles until abundant
it's spewed from hidden files;
Millions of bits of information,
Streaming in line by automation
to join the queue to bus the miles

Crafting, working against a set of deadlines
the solution emerges as columns of pencilled lines,
The time taken in design might seem funny,
but mistakes in this line of work cost money
Whizzing out more technological magic
My! How time flies, it's simply tragic.

Peter J McCafferty

TIME

How lonely it is;
The time of a day,
So many hours to pass away,
Minutes and seconds, the sound of a clock,
No key turning, no sound from the lock;
Alone with my thoughts, I sit in my chair,
Day turns to night, you're still not there;
No sound of your voice, no smile to see,
Just the sound of ticking endlessly;
Time is a killer, there is no doubt,
Time cannot heal what I am without;
Life goes on, or so they say,
My life is dying, day by day:
No-one else knows, only I can see,
How much I need you here with me;
My love keeps me going,
In the hope you'll be mine
I'll wait forever, till the end of time!

K Taylor

PRISON

The doors are locked, the windows barred,
Within these walls, souls are scarred,
As days drag on, hope is low,
The wheels of justice grind so slow,
But thoughts of home, so far away,
Help us to survive, day by day.
When at last, the gates open wide,
There's hope of a new life outside.

Stella R Corbett

SAVE OUR PLANET

Animals matter, yes they do,
They need to be wild, not in a zoo.
The have feelings like you and me,
Please don't hurt them, set them free!

Killing for ivory, fur and skin to wear
Is man really being fair?
Stop pollution, make the sea clean.
Don't use CFCs, please be green.

Animals are a pleasure to see
Protect them now for you and me.
If we don't, in years to come,
Our planet won't be much fun.
Our children will thank us for taking care.
And for protecting elephant, tiger and bear.

Once our forests were green and lush
Homes for animals of tree and bush
Then came man to lend a hand,
Chopping down trees, poisoning the land.
Now all we hear is Dutch elm and acid rain
When will our forests be green again?

Plant wild flowers, hedges and trees.
Bring back the wild life and the bees
Small trees one day will be,
Tomorrow's forests for you and me!

Denise Chappell

PROGRESS

The developer rubbed his hands in glee
And said 'I'd like you to come with me,
Out of town to where it once was green,
So you can share my greatest dream.'

We left the city and, out of town.
Were new ploughed fields with earth of brown.
'Now, what a waste of such a plot,
Think just what potential it has got!'

'People are just driving by.
Not one of them will stop to buy!'
'But there are no shops!' I remarked.
'That's just the trouble!' back he barked.

'Dream with me and I shall
Share my vision, my shopping mall!
When people drive out here to park
And go shopping - dawn to dark.'

'They'll be carried away with the need to spend;
Spend money, spend time, just spend.'
'It makes a nice day out,' they'll say,
'With the garden centre and shoppers' cafe'

Another new consumer amenity?
Or the newest way to avoid reality?
A pampered part of consumer boom,
A cocooned, heated shopping womb.

'But shops are for town and city.
To spoil green forest seems a pity.
The countryside is here for all to share,
Can't you see that you're being unfair?'

'You're missing the point, my naive lad,
Don't be so melancholy, or quite so sad.
Can't you see the seventh heaven
Of a mega-super-store on the A57?'

Christopher Brown

ALICE

When I close my eyes, I still can see
your round shiny face, and smell your
toothpaste breath upon my childhood cheek.
I miss the arms that would pull me
into your folds of love and security,
joking, laughing, soothing, you were always
the first to comfort my childish terrors.

Everyone loved you. They all wanted
a part of you, their selfish hands
pulling chunks of your essence, draining
your strength, beauty, life itself.

Sometimes your image is distorted in
my memories, children tend to do this
paint over the cracks with perfection
and pretence. But your radiance never
fades there. I used to bathe in the beauty
of your light but sometimes the queue was
long and I got left behind. But I forgive
you, but never them, they knew what they
were doing, I was a child unaware of the
frailties of life, mortality never existed
then, parents don't die.

Age hasn't healed the pain. The wound
still weeps as do I.
I look in the mirror and there you are,
a poor copy, but the only you I have now.

I try to live your chance but my flame
is weak. I can never burn as brightly
as you did, there are no queues around me.
But then you were unique and I am just
your daughter.

Trudi-Ann Handley

DEATH IN THE PAST

I stare up at the dismal grey tower,
My time has come, it is my hour.
The guard tugs and pulls me along,
I wish I could stay. I wish to belong.
My cries echo around the courtyard,
I tried to be brave, maybe too hard.
This life to me has been so unfair,
Not even one person seems to care.
They all tricked me into thinking it was right,
But when I was caught, they ran off in fright.
So here I stand about to die,
Just because I was honest and couldn't lie.
I stare up, at the sharpened blade,
And feel my pulse begin to fade,
As the blade comes crashing down,
I don't blink, not even a frown.
I feel the pain in a nauseous sweep,
Then begin to drift in a beautiful sleep.
I look down at my body as I float away,
And laugh at myself for wanting to stay.

T C Mountney

UNFINISHED POEM

Poetic spirit dying
Nowhere to call home
Words without a purpose
Title all alone
Life's long and winding story
Waiting to be told
Defective, uneventful
Searching for dissolve

Julie Sanderson

PEACE... N IRELAND, BOSNIA, AFRICA, IRAQ... AND SO MUCH MORE

Oh! Grant me the power to chastise man
For rape, desecration, of beauty and land
Whilst I sit on the hillside, in highlight and shade
The sun dropping low as the evening fades.

The birds homing flight with such beauty and ease
Searching each current of air and slight breeze
Whilst down in the valley stirs murmuring noise
Of man's false excitement, incitement and lies.

Our earth is so precious, and all freely given
Our years so numbered by patterns unknown
Let this be the time through the silence of sound
To offer our purpose, for new blessings unfound
The flickering of light through the sway of the leaves
The far distant mountains formed by millions of years

Yet man strives to conquer, to own, to destroy
To take from another, by threat or by ploy
such is his instinct, this being called man
Just when will he learn what his earth understands?

Oh! Grant me just once, this power I ask
To chastise mankind. Let this be my task.

John Horley

MOUNT OF VENUS

This heart lies weak and bleeding
Starved of love divine
Who stole the godly nectar?
Return to me what is mine
Our place was marble splendour
Amid woods, streams wreathed in cloud
Who let in Satan's apostle
Clothed in poisonous shroud?
I see the world below us
He may push, we cannot fall
For our ethereal fluid
Is not mortal at all

Vivien Thomas

THE LONELY OLD MAN

Sitting in his cottage near a roaring fire,
Keeping quiet and warm is his sole desire.
He is old and resigned to his fate,
He is weak and when walking, his legs will ache.

The country is quiet, no sound to be heard,
The snow is so thick, no song of a bird.
The lonely old man, he's just sitting there.
Asking himself, 'Why does nobody care?'

Irma Chester

TOMORROW

Come tomorrow, where will I be
And what will my mind be like?
Will it still be troubled and torn
And travelling on its usual hike?
Or will I feel better in a day or two -
Will I renew the same old feelings . . .?
Or will my heart be plummeting down
Or will it reach the ceiling?
Come tomorrow, what will I do?
And what if we happen to part?
Will I be unhappy with you
And still have my broken heart?
Or will I always love you -
Will I carry on as I have done -
Or will I say 'It's over,'
Or does tomorrow never come?
Come tomorrow, will I be sure
And what of the future to see -
Will I still want you around
And what if you don't want me?
Or will we be together still -
Will I see you - come what may?
Or will we see what tomorrow brings
Or will we call it a day?

I Cone

OH FATHER

Oh Father, please help me, for this I can't ignore.
I've just received bad news and feel I can't live any more.
I'd like to know the reason this condition is with me,
I can't accept why I should be so different, you see.

I've always led my life so full, I want it to remain,
I'm trying to come to terms with it before I go insane.
Things won't be the same and time will tell if I adjust,
For me and all my loved ones, I realise I must.

And now I am dependent on something to survive
That's governed by the time each day and food to stay alive.
I'm hoping that the time will come to rid me of this sin
And stop myself from taking artificial insulin.

But now some time has been and gone since starting on this course,
I must admit it doesn't seem as bad as I first thought.
Now I don't regret so much the things I left behind
It's just that I can't get the bloody needle off my mind.

But now some more time has elapsed,
I've grown to see the light
It's not so bad injecting every morning, noon and night.
There're others far worse off than me, I'm certain I won't fail
For the one thought keeps me going
I'm alive to tell the tale.

Malcolm Mayo

WHERE EMPTY MEANS FULL

The past is a place without a name
A scrolling lost shroud in mist fades white
Ice crystal snow laced
Like doom beating drums for the coast

A road and mountain and emptiness abound
I am a door in the shaping of reality
A solid ghost of futures
Like peeling back my skin to find a universe

No stranger to denial, with no way to cry
A fast land weaved with sorrow
Spreading overtones politely
Like I tell you a dark tale, because you are light

I excel in beginning things which remain unfinished
Striking out on expeditions, disconnection
Sordid eyes that do not lie - and do not tell the truth
Like saplings are not trees, strictly speaking

On the edge looking in towards nothing
Hearing only the memory of belief in sound
The taste of power
Like a hole in the whole of a book, or a brick on a page.

Nick Williams

I'M A BIG GIRL NOW

It's time I had my say now, Mum,
I'm old enough to speak my mind.
You still see me as a little girl,
So, please Mum, don't be blind.

Look at me, I'm a big girl now,
Don't tell me to be quiet.
I want your opinion, not a row.
Don't let me be so defiant.

There are days when you say, 'Please shut up,'
You have no time for me.
You are only interested in your affairs
Talking to a friend that's come to tea.

Mum, I am a teenager now,
I can think for myself.
So please, oh please, will you listen
For I'll always need your help.

All I want is a simple answer
To a question I want to ask.
'Is it all right if I wear some make-up
Now that I'm not a child at last.'

Jean Lloyd Williams

COOKING UP TROUBLE

When the clotted cream of life runs down a jammy chin onto your
                                                                                                best gown;
and every currant problem seems like a gooseberry fool to all
                                                                                                 your dreams;
Try not to care if soufflés don't rise, or ice cream melts in front
                                                                                               of your eyes;
if seed cake crumbles when breadcrumbs don't, and butter runs
                                                                                      when icing won't.
Even though your pies won't puff, and shortcrust pastry turns
                                                                                            out rough;
when mincemeat describes the state of your life, and is twice
                                                                        as dull as your best kitchen knife.
'Cos you're not the only one in the stew, it's tripe to imagine
                                                                           it's only you.
Everybody's lives are scrambled from the time they leave the shell.
They go through murky mulligatawny, clear consommé as well.

But occasionally there comes a thyme when pork is served
                                                                                with stuffing.
It melts in your mouth like nothing else, and you feel you want
                                                                             for nothing.

So it seems we only stay in the soup until we learn to cope
with life's occasional custard pies, and don't sit there and mope.

Carol Smith

RED

Carnations red, a bridegroom's wedding
Farewell to the dead, the tears we're shedding
Flanders' fields with poppies growing
A reddish dawn, a cockerel crowing
No time for life, no time for joy
A nation's freedom, in the hands of a boy
No time to question, no time to lie
Just time to think, just time to die.

M J Hughes

MY MUM

I have this poem, just for my mum.

L ove we all need, and fun times too.
O ur smiles, tell us we're happy not blue.
V anish my pain when I cry, please, mum,
E nd my tears with a cuddle and some.

Y oghurt perhaps when I want something to eat,
O ur play times may in the end leave you beat.
U ntil it's time for my wash, and then off to bed,

M um then it's your time, so you can clear your head.
U sually, I don't always remember to say I care,
M um, *I love you,* lots and lots, *so there.*

A Brenda Original

THE WARNING

This little speck which wanders through space.
And is the home of the human race,
Was meant to be by the mighty one,
A garden of Eden, joy and fun.
But man has chosen the path of sin,
Instead of following and believing in Him.
If man does not begin to alter his ways,
For his mistakes and errors must he pay,
Man in his folly to quickly progress,
With the laws of nature has made such a mess,
The seas' and oceans' waters of absolution,
Are now saturated with toxic pollution,
The forests and plains, once full of life,
Are now scenes of war and strife,
The clean sweet air that once we knew,
Is now the blessing of very few
If we do not this world cherish,
In years to come, it will surely perish,
We have to live by the laws he gave
If the human race we are to save.

J Sharp

MOVING

The house is soon empty, and mum sits alone,
Unfurnished and hollow, my home is no more.
Bare rooms and bare walls, no longer my own,
Memories like rubbish are kicked to the floor.
Did they say we were moving? I don't recall
Packed off to my nan's, kept out of the way.
Loose papers and boxes all over the hall
The memory fades - the old place is grey.
Presents from neighbours as they say goodbye.
We're starting once more, and leaving this place
Boxes and blankets, the car was piled high
A new world, a new home, we now had to face.
As we left this life, old neighbours grew thin
A new world awaits, a world to begin.

Amy Bennett

A ROSE

As snow is melting on the ground
When earth is shedding her bridal gown
What mysteries lie beneath the soil
of a garden tended with loving care
When summer comes around and fills the air
with gentle breezes, we stop and stare
Red, yellow, pink and white
Glistening with dew in the morning light
A heavenly fragrance will reach us at night
Petals curled in sweet repose
a beauty so rare
Beyond compare
is that of the lovely English rose!

Margaret Appleyard

THE CHILDREN OF DUNBLANE

It's hard for us our thoughts to say
The horror of that mid-March day
When one mad gunman took away
The children of Dunblane

Most of us can't realise
The agony when our child dies
Or cry the tears those parents cried
For the children of Dunblane

I only hope at that bad time
A host of angels stood in line
And said just put your hand in mine
To the children of Dunblane

D Hester

POLLUTION

Often comes the warning
Danger from global warming.
Stop greenhouse gas emissions.
Industry adding to conditions.
We have little say
Way things are today
They must have profit
We can't stop it!

Many give their blessing
Believing it's only guessing.
Waiting to be burned
Before they are concerned

Drought and floods abound
Causing horror all around
This man made pollution
Giving us no solution.

But try, we can,
To make a ban.
To give less woe
Pollution then must go.

James Brockbank

DEAREST NIECE

Her cheeky smile, and deep blue eyes
so much joy,
I'm so glad she's not a boy.

Oh so pretty, oh so sweet,
now she's crawling at my feet.

A footstep, a stride, and then a tumble,
what was that I heard her mumble?

The way she walks, and tries to talk,
is a constant source of much delight,
I only hope she sleeps tonight.

Out with the light,
asleep at night,
I wish you pleasant dreaming.
close your eyes, no more screaming.

A beauty to behold, a life to unfold.
There she goes with that toddling manner
what a joy, my niece called Hannah.

David Carress

AN OBSESSION

Chocolate I have to say is definitely my obsession,
I try to blame it on something, possibly depression,
Always dieting, wishing I was lovely and thin,
No matter what I do, my obsession will always win,
I look at myself in the mirror my huge stomach, legs and bum,
All I end up doing is wishing I wasn't so dumb,
I cry and shout saying, 'No more, this is it,'
But when tomorrow comes , I think what the hell, and have another bit,
At the moment I'm fairly young, but I want to be old and grey,
The way I'm going now, I'll never make it to see that day,
If I do make it I know, if I carry on eating with such intensity,
I'll be unhealthy, unfit and I'm sure well into obesity,
I've decided I'm going to really try and get a new thin me,
Tomorrow's another day so we'll have to wait and see!

Jayne Wherritt

TIME

The inventions of man that bring him power appear
his density for them to flower.

His nuclear power and the threat of his bomb, we
must admit are very strong.

But the strongest force, its fuel is change that no
man can move or disarrange.

Or even hope or attempt to stop, is the simple tick
of the clock.

For with each tick, his power and he, will surely one
day cease to be.
Such men of war, may one day achieve their aims,
But only for a while for time will take away their smile.

'To be or not to be? is the question, a quote that's rather
sentimental.

To do or not to do is far more fundamental

These men fail to grasp the sweetest thing,
it's value greater than anything, is life.

John Winston-Smith

THE BIRTHDAY HOUR

Take heart from this, the birthday hour
You're still a bud, not yet a flower.

Soon time will flee, it's cruel but true
The bloom will fade and lose its hue.

Petals fall to frost's wintry grip
The rose you were becomes the hip.

So waste no time this birthday morn
For all too soon, no rose, just thorn.

Gary Walmsley

CHRISTMAS

Be still,
Be very still
Or you will miss again
The sweep of angels' wings,
The babe's faint cry.
It is for you He calls
For you, He comes.
Oh, lay your heart
This starlight time
Within his tiny nail-pierced hands,
And do not wait . . .
Until the next year,
Or the next.

Beth Roberts

A CHILD'S BEDTIME PRAYER

Wrap me up in your love, Lord,
Tuck me in with your care
Send a baby angel
To help me say my prayer
Be a blanket enfolding
Little me through the night.
Switch on a tiny star, Lord,
To shine on me till morning light.

Then when morning has come, Lord,
And the sun comes out to peek.
Let there be a sunbeam
To kiss me on my cheek
Don't let go of my hand, Lord,
Stay by me through the day
And guard me as your treasure
Whether at school or play

Bless my mum and my dad, Lord.
And all my family
In the palm of your hand, Lord,
You carved them all
As you carved me
I'm so happy to know, Lord,
How much you cherish us all,
The big, strong, grown-up people
And those like me, so very small,
You love us all.

Win Slater

POSTIES

Aren't our posties wonderful!
They turn out in all weathers
Even if it's cold or hot
They bring our cards and letters.

They always seem so cheerful
I've never seen them sad,
They get up at the crack of dawn
For some that would be bad.

They don't all drive a nice warm van
Some have to ride a bike
Or trudge the streets on foot
This can be quite a hike.

So when you have a nice lie-in
And you hear the letterbox 'tat'
Then dash downstairs and say 'Hello'
To your friendly Postman Pat.

Delma Bruce

A MOTHER IN MIND

How I wish I still had my mother
I know she would have been very proud of me
Many times when I'm sat alone
I think of the days when I was young
When my mother held me on her knee
With all the love in her heart for my brother and I
She meant everything to us
I wish the children of today would love their parents
In every way, not leave home without a word
Because they thought they had not been heard
Think of the good things and the happy times you could all have
Together before you make this tragic decision
Try to understand your mother's position
Stay by her side, think again, save all the worry and the pain
That comes into her mind while you're away
There's no other can take her place
There is no-one like your own mother.

Edna Ball

AUTUMN AND WINTER WINDS

The lovely October days are ending
The warmth has gone from the sun
The wind has begun to whistle
And moan down the chimney for fun
He's blowing the leaves from the trees now
Scattering them far and wide
Hither and thither they swirl around
And then just for a moment he may bide
Before he sets off to blow down the lanes
And blow under our doors and rattle the panes
Of all the windows and swirl off again
Blowing the washing of every Mary and Jane
The berries are red now - the holly all out
The children now excited and all starting to shout
'It's Hallowe'en - it's Bonfire Night!'
As off they go on those windy nights
Spooks and fireworks matter not
To our autumn winds we have now got
With us till Christmas - and then comes the snow
Out on their sledges they all will go
He'll blow himself out - for a little while
And when we begin to think, spring, and smile
'Those March winds doth blow
And we shall have snow'
So the old rhyme tells us so
But in like a lion - out like a lamb
The seasons go on and perhaps we can
Forget all the wind - and think of the sun
And autumn and winter winds have all had their fun!

Nora Billington

POOR DADDY LONG LEGS

I've got six legs much finer than glass,
I'm Daddy long legs, I fly so fast.
I was so thirsty I needed a drink,
So I flew into the kitchen sink.
I'm going, I'm going, I'm not very strong,
And down the drain I've quickly gone.

Perhaps I'll swim right out to sea,
Or this might be the end of me.

Kay Clements

THE STREETS OF LONDON

To walk the streets of London,
As night-time closes in.
There you will see young and old,
With nowhere else to go.

Left out on a cold dark night,
No warm bed or food to eat!
Living on a cold damp street.
Inside doorways, under arches,
Lying in boxes where they sleep.

Come rain or snow the terrible cold,
They suffer in silence,
Or, are they just bold,
To suffer all this and beat the cold?

If only they could all have homes,
With somewhere warm to go.
Have a place of work so they could eat,
That would be a real treat!
To know they wouldn't be left on the street,
Warm slippers for their weary feet.
And a clean, warm bed where they could sleep.

Will these comforts ever be theirs?
Will we, as humans, ever learn to care?

Margaret Hughes

BIG TED

My best friend is Teddy
I cuddle him at night
And when I'm feeling lonely
I hold him very tight
He always, always loves me
So I think you will agree
If Teddy had a best friend
It would probably be me.

J E Goulding

THE WAITING GAME

I cry within as I close the door
For my love has gone to war
I asked of him 'Take care,'
Life's just not being fair.
Why did he have to go to war?

My thoughts of how we were before
brings smiles to my face once more.
But smiles won't last I am aware
I cry within

Time passes slowly, thoughts are raw,
The waiting game becomes a bore.
In search of headlines, I dare,
to see if your name is written there.
Anguish, relent, outpour.
I cry within.

Kathleen Johnson

PLATONIC FRIENDSHIP

I must have known it first in the springtime
I knew it the same in the end
That you and your love were plighted
Why couldn't you just be my friend?

Couldn't we sit in the twilight
Couldn't we walk by the shore
With only a pleasant friendship
To bind us and nothing more?

We touched on so many subjects
The moon and the stars above
But our conversation was scientific
There was never a mere hint of love

I have fought with my heart and conquered
I have hidden my wound from sight
You were going away in the morning
So I had to say a very calm goodnight

But now as I sit in the twilight
Or when I stroll by the sea
That friendship, quite platonic
Still comes surging over me

Mary Elizabeth Bridges

I JUST WANTED TO

I just want to thank you
For being you
If you weren't around
I don't know what I'd do
You've always been there for me
Through the good times and the bad
You've shown me understanding
When I've been really sad
You do not judge nor criticise
You do not interfere
You're someone I can talk to
You chase away my fear
I just want to say 'I love you'
And thank you for all you've done
You're a very special person
And I'm glad that you're my mum.

Jenny Betchley

I LOVE YOU STILL

I love you still, though you have gone
My love for you yet lingers on
I now have learned you do not care
And go your way, quite unaware
The sun is dark, where once it shone.

The face I lived to look upon
Has vanished as the stars at dawn
My bitter pain I cannot bear
I love you still.

I saw you as the paragon
As lovely as the graceful swan
But now my world is bleak and bare
And all my castles in the air
Are empty dreams - oblivion!
I love you still.

Ralph McMurray

HEAVEN'S VERY SPECIAL CHILD

A meeting was held quite far from earth.
It's time again for another birth,
Said the angels to the Lord above
This special child will need much love
Her progress may seem very slow
Accomplishments she may not show
And she'll require extra care
From all the folks she meets down there
She may not run or laugh or play
Her thoughts may seem quite far away
In many ways he won't adapt
And she'll be known as handicapped
So let's be careful where she's sent
We want her life to be content
Please Lord, find parents who
Who will do a special job for you
They will not realise right away
The leading role they're asked to play
But with this child sent from above
Comes stronger faith and richer love
And soon they'll know the privilege given
In caring for this gift from heaven
Their precious charge, so meek and mild
Is heaven's very special child.

G L Crowe

PSALM OF HOPE

If my tears are kept in a bottle,
how large it must be,
And is there a scale that can weigh my grief?
Does the sound of my anguish
echo around the courts of heaven,
where some angelic scribe writes
my prayers on the heavenly reams?

But hush my soul, be still.
Consider the Lord your God.
Is He the divine torturer,
goading you beyond endurance,
or is He the God of all comfort?
Didn't you pray to be more like Christ?
Rejoice that your prayers have been answered,
for He is working out His sovereign will in your life,
That you may know patience, confidence and trust.

Brenda Finegan

WHEN

When race can embrace race and forge a bond,
To banish hatred to a frontier far beyond.
And with each step, from darkness into light,
Together, without fear, defend the right.

When we can laugh in moments of despair,
And tip the scales when judging is not fair,
And weigh each day the losses and the gains,
Contented with whichever one remains.

When we can care for both the young and old,
Encourage strays back to the social fold.
And sorrow knocking gently at your door,
Think of those whose heartaches are much more.

When we can pledge life's gains with hidden deed,
Make people think of love, instead of greed,
And pressing forward in some earthly race,
Be kind to those who cannot keep the pace.

When waste of human conflict has been solved,
And peaceful progress is at last resolved,
When we can conquer all these many things,
There'll be peace on earth, and all the joy it brings.

Thomas Victor Healey

GOLDEN HEART ENTWINE

Oh the soul of the mere mortal cries into the night
Fill my soul with love and warm sweet surrender.
Shall be the night's voice spoken into thy heart.
For never again shall thy soul encounter such love
That can rage the swirling seas from the calm.

Stirring all the passion from the soul in thee.
Take on to thee thy love, joy and happiness
Love is a word that enters thy soul and mind
Within giving the inner feelings to thoughts.

When the mind and soul feel thy harmony
They then become one within thee. Yes the one
The one thing that bonds a man and woman
The power of love is within thy soul, heart, mind

Heaven and moonlit skies, sandy beaches.
Capture the soul into celestial bliss
A tear falls into the ocean blue, true blue
A wave wraps around the soul Oh such bliss

The sweet divine taste of the most whitest wine
Wets the lips with nectar from the heavens
Pouring down 100 scented rose petals
With the sweet scent of virtue, to love

Oh heavenly God, sweet divine majestic regime
Thy hath blessed thy mortal with love so supreme
A golden arrow across it seen
The locked golden heart entwine has been.

Rhonda Russell

GHOST SHIPS

Those mighty oaken ships sailed long ago,
To the icy lands across the heaving sea.
Guided by the ghostly sentinels so strong.
The raging wind echoed their Danish song.
Bloodthirsty barbarians born of bone and steel.

Scott Turner

UNTITLED

As you sit today round your table,
Daddy, mummy and children,
Spare a thought for the broken family,
Who are not able to share a meal,
Is it mummy who's gone, who knows where,
Or daddy who no longer can care.
That makes this family broken.

In your own little private castle,
Where your family surrounds you with love,
Spare a thought for the daddy or mummy,
Who has all the care and hassle
Of loving and feeding as best they can
With the little that is given.

When you see your own children behaving
As all good children should,
Spare a thought for 'those naughty, noisy children'
Whose daddy or mummy has left.
Oh why do you act so smug?

They only need a friendly word
Or just to sit on your knee,
Just a cuddle or a kiss so that they do not miss
The daddy or mummy who has gone.
Just try to remember that it's not their fault
That they don't realise what's going on.
All they have is a memory that hurts
Of a daddy or mummy who's gone.

Kathleen Jarvis

A PLACE

There is in a course of a day,
Guidance, truth and love,
We know of all these things,
As they are sent from Heaven above,

Now! Heaven is such a beautiful place,
Where love does conquer all,
And Heaven holds a place for you
When it's time to hear your Father's call,

His voice is soft and gentle,
His words most sincere,
You will feel the warmth that's near Him,
When you get so very near,

As when you leave this time on earth,
And gone up to your home above,
You won't believe the feeling there,
It's just filled with love,

So when you think of your time on earth,
And that you are afraid to die,
Never ever be afraid my friends,
As you spirit will be set free to fly.

Jessica Wright

BURDEN OF PROOF

From the burden of proof,
The Tabernacle burns,
It burns religion into the soul,
And preaches damnation without the cross,
Perpetuated by feeding on children's fears,
It sweeps across undiscovered lands,
Ranting its benefits without consideration,
Bringing not only God but pestilence, disease and plague,
God's divine retribution.
It stands up for the poor, weak and homeless,
But still hoards its fortunes of conversion,
Hangs a cloak of respectability over its sexuality,
While whipping up fervour for holy wars,
So has religion got sanctity?
Or is it just sanctimonious?
Perhaps God should have no religion.

Timm Dorsett

SOMEONE DOES CARE

When life seems empty with nowhere to go
Your heart is troubled and spirits are low
When friends seem so few and none seem to care
There is always God who will hear your prayer.

Whatever you're facing will seem so much less
If you can confide and also confess
The burden that once seemed too much to bear
God lifts away on the wings of prayer
And then in the stillness of your own mind
New born assurance you will surely find
Someone will answer
Someone does care
There will be an answer
To each sincere prayer.
Many just pray that their troubles will cease
Then without effort, they'll win carefree peace.
To pray for more courage is much better trend
God often answers by way of a friend . . .

Ellen Hall

THE CYCLE OF TIME

In spring the buds
Burst forth again
Growing and blooming
In the soft gentle rain

In summertime the days are long
And birds on wing are
Full of song
And flowers are blossoming everywhere
Life is easy and free
From care

In autumn the
Air smells of bonfires
And the leaves fall
From the trees
Browns, ambers and gold
Flutter along on the breeze

In winter the trees
Are stark and bare
The howling wind
Is the only sound
And silent snowflakes
Cover the ground.

Heather Brown

FOREVER

Though your feet no longer tread
Upon this earthly plane
They now walk by sparkling lakes
And wander leafy lanes.

For you can see a world unknown
To loved ones, you must depart
All pain and suffering now has flown
Peace, wondrous fills your heart.
I see you bathed in glorious light
Reclothed in body new
A radiant smile upon your face
Your feet in gentle dew.

I see you walking on God's sacred hills
And through His valleys green
In a land that we cannot yet know
To our mortal eyes unseen.
Touched by a myriad of rainbows
You walk the blue beyond
Where golden light dispels the shadows
And darkness is unknown.

Though your years on earth
Were but a few
In our hearts, your footprints stay
And when our time on earth is done
We'll meet again, someday.
We shed tears at your passing
But the power of love is such
Though we can't follow
Where you tread
You still walk on earth, with us.

Jessica Jordan

FOR WHAT WE ARE ABOUT TO RECEIVE

Happily pondering . . . like a gourmet selects
His favourite dish, such sybaritic whim,
Anticipating gastronomic effects
Of integral parts contributing to the whole
Creation, undoubtedly so cuisine-correct
In every detail. Perfection as the goal
Boosted by a most exquisite bouquet, -
Breath of Bacchus a bard could well extol,
Enchantment to the culinary creation.
Cognac-cooked through casserole and pan,
Inciting buds of taste its motivation
And Epicurean ecstasy in man;
Redolent of the flavour of some clove,
Perhaps a most delectable Coq au Vin . . .
Happily pondering, in paths of gourmets strove,
In lunch-hour brief, to savour salad roll.

Mary Ryan

I Didn't Know You Jesus

I didn't know You Jesus
but still You cared for me.
I didn't know that You had died
for me at Calvary.
I didn't know that You had shed
Your blood to set me free.
I didn't know You Jesus
until I came to see.

I didn't love You Jesus
yet Your love was so deep.
You watched me every waking hour
and blessed each night of sleep.
Though every time I let You down
it must have made You weep.
You always counted me dear Lord
when You were counting sheep.

I didn't praise You Jesus
when others spoke Your name.
When things were going wrong Lord
You often took the blame.
And yet despite my attitude
You loved me just the same,
and when I called You Jesus
straight to my side You came.

Yes, now I know You Jesus,
the friend whom I ignored.
I couldn't love You more now.
Each day You are adored.
In You I am made perfect,
through You I am restored.
I didn't know or love or praise.
Forgive me my dear Lord.

John Christopher

PIPE OF PEACE

He smiled, but never spoke,
She had chips, in a poke,
Never seen this, ever before,
So, he had a treat in store,
Indian Chief from far away,
In Glasgow, for the day,
She offered, with help yourself,
He enjoyed them, she could tell,
Licked his fingers, got out his pipe,
She disappeared into the night.
Didn't want to smoke, the Pipe of Peace,
After her chip and vinegar feast.

Dinah Matthew

SUCK A LEMON!

Desire was a lemon
With a scent so fresh and clean
Its golden skin so smooth
With an exotic taste to glean.

Oh, how I pursed my lips
At just one morsel of this fruit
No sweetness, for its sour juice
Revealed it as a brute.

Kim Montia

FEATHERS

The gift of the eider,
A soft and downy quilt,
An ostrich in contrast,
Has feathers that wilt.
The peacock's proud eye
Shows in his spread tail,
While the sportsman takes
Fancy to pheasant and quail.
Aloft in the heavens
A great eagle soars,
And a darting blue bird,
Behind the waterfall's roar.
Softly, the barn owl
Glides in on her flight,
With silent destruction,
Of mice by moonlight.
Feathered wonders of nature,
For mankind to share,
The unsurpassed masters,
Of life in the air.

Zoë Ford

WHAT IS IT?

You can't smell it, tell it, buy or even sell it
Use it, abuse it, hide or ever lose it.
People try to box it, others to out-fox it.
No matter what you do, it will always stay with you.
Where you go it follows, always at your side
On hills or down in hollows, there is nowhere you can hide.
Usually at their best, in sunshine at the park
Sometimes can be frightening, especially in the dark.
They mix will all the peasants, or a king upon his throne
Everyone can see them, they are never on their own.
Every person has one, no matter what their size
Sometimes they just disappear, and you don't realise.
No-one else can meet him, only if you're there
But if you ever greet him, people stand and stare.
If they drive you crazy, don't say I told you so,
Just take a look a others, alone with their shadow . . .

GIG

THE MALE PERSPECTIVE

The sky is grey and murky, storm clouds riding high.
His life is turgid and sullen, like the swollen sky.
His suit, so immaculate. Now creased and rumpled.
A physical reminder of plans that have crumbled.

He has to be strong. The Leader. It's what his job requires.
Yet inside his stomach is churning. His mind easily tires.

His dreams are now tattered. It's written on his face.
For those who care to read them, all his misery trace.
His house is like an empty box, where once his children ran.
A feeling of isolation fills this lonely man.

He looks into the mirror, sees anger in his eyes.
Not directed at the world outside,
But at something deep inside.
He should have recognised the evidence.
Seen his marriage fall apart.
His wife's increasing bitterness.
His own slowly breaking heart.

His work had ruled his existence.
For his family he had no time.
Now solitary confinement,
The punishment for his crime.

He holds no hopes for the future.
He dwells painfully in the past.
All his memories he tends to nurture.
Recounting what he's lost.

Everyday seems like a battle.
Each evening a victory is won.
Serving another part of his sentence.
Yet parole for him. There is none.

Christine George

EACH DAY AS OUR LAST

We only did what we had to do to survive,
    But now there's nowhere left for us to run or hide.
We were never gonna let 'em take us alive,
    Gone in a blaze of glory like Bonnie and Clyde.
Our names to be remembered and romanticised,
    Our faces to adorn T-shirts worn with fierce pride.
They branded us outlaws but society lied,
    Lynch mobs found us guilty without us being tried.
Not our fault we happened to be on the wrong side,
    Where were you the day teenage rebellion died?

Danny Kember

EXCUSES

Excuses I have heard them all,
As to why they can't accept the saviours call.
I'm too busy getting right to the top,
I've got to meet some rich old clot,
Who is as thick as two short planks.
I'll bear in mind what you've said and thanks
Alas it will not enter her head
again today.
She will be happily on her way.
Oblivious to the fact today will be
The last day on earth she will see.
For the old clot does drink and drive,
And today to her he will lie.
He will say he has not touched a drop.
But she said he was a clot.
Into his sports car she did climb,
Now she was going down the line.
In the wreckage they're both found,
And for hell both were bound.
Jesus stood beside the wreckage of the car,
But neither of them realised how far
The saviour had gone to set them free
From their sins at Calvary.
They rejected him, they did not want to know.
And you reap just what you sow.

Don Goodwin

TONIGHT MY WORDS FALL LIKE RAIN
(For Maria)

Tonight my words fall like rain. My heart, the cloud, has burst.
The night is shattered and scattered like a million stars . . .

She is in the distance. And the distance is eternal.

The cold wind whistles and sings. Her sweet voice calls to me.
It is a sad and lonesome melody that comes to haunt my ears.

I love her even now. And so, my words come easily.
And when these saddest words have ceased she may love me.

Now, through nights like this my arms are empty.
And my kisses are hers only in my dreams.

Once, I looked into her deep dark eyes.
And I knew my heart was mine no more.

Gone. Like grains of sand slipping through my fingers.

And like the verse the rain falls as intensely as my words.
Without her to hear, they are swept away on an endless river.

This night and every other night.

The distance is eternal.
The song is from the soul.

She is not with me now. Yet she is with me.
So I will search forever because she owns my heart.

We, of this time can be the same.

I love her. That is certain. And if I whisper the words, 'I love you.'
I will pray to the breeze to carry them to her ears.

I know she is anothers. Her face. Her eyes. Her body.
But if she desires, my kisses are hers, only hers.

I love her. That I know. Maybe she loves me. I do not know.
I cannot forget. I cannot pretend. Love is strong.

Now, through nights like this my arms are empty.
Through nights like this my soul is restless.

I know this pain is endless and that I suffer through her silence.
In my silence I love her. That is certain.

These words I write because of her. And through my words I will suffer more.

This I know. This is certain. This and every other night.

John Dewar

WHEN SOMEONE DIES
(In Memory Of My Granddad, John Frederick Miles)

When someone dies tears fill my eyes,
And sadness takes its place in my soul,
Nothing seems right as I cry all through the night,
Knowing someone has gone through a dark hole.

Days go past, nothing has changed,
Days go past, everything's the same,
My only wish is for you to be happy,
But at the same time please, still think of me.

I know you're leading a happy life,
I will still think of you in my every strife,
You do know,
You did not have to go.

Hajar Javaheri (11)

REMEMBER...

We wear our poppies in pride,
For the graves stand side by side.
The word is remember,
On the 11th of November.

The red maybe for blood,
The silent bodies in the mud,
The black may be for doom,
The bodies in their unknown tomb.

Matthew Allen

FIRESTORM

White-hot lasers bounce off my shields,
They are beginning to lose power.
Lifeless and cold for all eternity,
Space like the darkest ink is waiting.
One fatal mistake, one tiny error,
Will see me expelled into the void.
Tiny drops of sweat fall from my brow,
As I frantically twist and turn.
My battleship is pushed to its limit,
Until I have shaken off my pursuer.
Then like a swooping eagle,
In pursuit of its prey I close in.
My enemy is unaware he is now hunted,
With full power to my lasers I fire.
His fatal mistake, his tiny error,
Has sent him into the void for all eternity.

I love the cinema.

Paul Willis

THE BEST THINGS IN LIFE

The best things in life
Are the things that are free
The love of one's husband
And family.

The people I've met
The friends I've made
As years go on
I reassure them
Like a beautiful song.

I love good music
Song and dance
Those are the things
'I think'
That make life worth while.

One should always
Try to smile
Life is too short
To be miserable and glum.

So shake a leg
And have some fun.

Catherine Wigglesworth

QUESTIONS, AND THE REASONS WHY
(A Door-man's perspective) (For Hannah)

He had taken a few blows,
From his fellow drunk,
But paid them back with interest,
His adrenaline was still flowing,
He felt no pain,
Never . . . Any . . . Pain.
(It was written there, on his knuckles).

His girl had left before the bouts conclusion,
Why did she show no concern?
What if the doorman had raised his opponents' hand in victory?
What then eh? . . . Eh?
After all,
He was protecting her honour,
(The way he was looking at her),
What was he supposed to do?
He knew that look all-right.

My goodness,
Was she lucky to have found him,

Women, eh?

I ask you,

I ask you.

Simon Green

BRITISH DISEASE

'British disease' said the humanist,
'Is what you must expect.
If a poet's true assessment,
Is what you've learned to give respect.'

'British basics, are the values,
You will get from Mr Blair,
God, Queen and Aristocracy,
But all else will be nowhere.'

Do not hope for human welfare,
And pacification of the world,
When the part-world diplomatic flags
Are by Blair unfurled.

You will get massive defence spending
For international support,
With tender tax for billionaires,
And lotteries the newest sport.

But behold the bulging prisons,
And the 'madness' on TV,
Tough on crime? You're joking,
It is just *wrong sociology.*

Edward Graham Macfarlane

ROBIN

The robin said to Jenny wren
It's nice to see you back again
I've known that I would have to wait
To see you on the garden gate.
Last time I saw you it was snowing
I never knew where you were going.
I seem to meet you once a year
Because you go abroad I fear.
But you appear on Christmas cards
So I am working very hard
To help the Christmas season through
So I send my regards to you.

Mary Tickle

THE DARK HORSE

Tom, a country lad both born and bred,
whom locals thought soft in the head.
But soon these folks would get to know,
That our lad Tom was not so slow.
He studied books near the country paths,
And soon became quite good at maths.
The lad was keen you must give due,
For he mastered other subjects too.
He applied and joined a local college,
Where he surprised the tutors with his knowledge.
They discussed his work and their recommendation,
Was Tom was suited for a higher education.
It was off to Uni Tom did go,
And from his pen great works did flow.
And Tom on whom those folks did frown,
Became a scholar of great renown.
There's a lesson here to rediscover,
Like a book don't judge one by the cover.

L Heatley

THE GREEN LADY

We sailed past Liberty island
close to the lady etched in green,
on our way towards the New World
towards a happier scene.
Then onto the harbour, and the milling crowd
waiting on the quay.
We were full of excitement
at the fresh wonders we would see,
in this new land, so full of promise,
of hope, as yet unfulfilled.
So now we step down onto new ground.
It was as the Good Lord had willed.
We left, far behind that dark land
of great fear, and taloned hawk
to find our bright new future
on these streets of Old New York.

Gordon B Bannister

INFORMATION

We hope you have enjoyed reading this book - and that you will continue to enjoy it in the coming years.

If you like reading and writing poetry drop us a line, or give us a call, and we'll send you a free information pack.

Write to :-
**Triumph House Information
1-2 Wainman Road
Woodston
Peterborough
PE2 7BU
(01733) 230749**